Grandma and Aqelesiya Look for Birds

A Nature Adventure!

Linda Dillon deJong

AuthorHouse™
1663 Liberty Drive
Bloomington, IN 47403
www.authorhouse.com
Phone: 1 (800) 839-8640

Published by AuthorHouse 04/10/2019

ISBN: 978-1-5462-7921-1 (sc)
ISBN: 978-1-5462-7920-4 (e)

Library of Congress Control Number: 2019901340

Printed in the United States of America.

This book is printed on acid-free paper.

authorHOUSE®

TABLE OF CONTENTS

DEDICATION

This book is dedicated to my beautiful little Ethiopian granddaughter Aqelesiya. My son came from Ethiopia as a teenager. He attended all four years of high school here in the USA where he was the star of his soccer team. After he grew up, he visited Ethiopia and became reacquainted with his middle school sweetheart. He visited Ethiopia several times to court his girlfriend who was attending college there. After many months our son was able to obtain a "Fiancé Visa" to bring his beautiful bride to the USA. They were married in Everett, Washington, and had a beautiful daughter Aqelesiya. When she is older I hope Aqelesiya wants to look for birds with Grandma! I hope that she will always keep her sense of wonder!

Grandma lives on Camano Island. First Aqelesiya goes across the bridge to get onto Camano Island.

Aqelesiya sees the Welcome to Camano Island sign.

This is Grandma. She is so happy to see Aqelesiya!

It is a nice winter day on Camano Island. It is a good time to look for birds that are traveling from their summer home to their winter home. This is called migration.

Why is that field white?

It is full of birds!

They are Snow Geese!

This is a farm near Mount Vernon, Washington.

The birds are traveling, and they stop to eat and rest.
They eat the little plants in the field.
The gray birds are babies.

The Snow Geese are so hungry!
They flew a long way to get here!

Now they are taking off! Wow!

Can you hear them all saying "Honk, Honk?"

Snow Geese come here in the winter.

In the summer they go way up north to the Arctic where they make nests and raise their baby geese called goslings.

They are so beautiful!
They have black tips on their wings.

Goodbye! Have a safe trip!

Now Grandma and Aqelesiya arrive at the water. This is near Anacortes, Washington.
That is Mount Baker with new snow on top!

Look at these pretty American Widgeon ducks! The boy ducks have a green stripe on their heads, the girls have a brown head.

There are some Northern Pintail ducks! The boys have a white stripe on their neck, and the girl ducks are brown.

Oh Aqelesiya! I see a big eagle nest up in that tree!

Look! There is a Bald Eagle!
His head and tail are white.

Oh! He is going to fly away! His wings are so big!

You can see his white tail when he is flying.
Goodbye Mr. Eagle!

Look Aqelesiya! There is a Blue Heron!

He has a long neck.

Now he is flying away. Look how big his wings are!

Look Aqelesiya! There is another Blue Heron standing by the water!

Look, now the Blue Heron is flying over the water! You can see his long neck is curved like the letter S.

Look Aqelesiya! That bird swimming is a young Cormorant! He will dive under the water to eat a fish!

Now the Cormorant is flying!

Look Aqelesiya! There are some Canada Geese!
They are mostly brown with a black head and a white
stripe under the chin. The girls and boys look the same.

Oh Look! Now they are flying to the water!

The Canada Geese are landing on the water!

Look! Now they are swimming with the ducks!

Oh Look! There is a Mallard Duck with a green head. The girl duck likes him and follows him.

The girl is still following him. He is not sure he likes her, so he flies away.

She looks around and says, "Where did my boyfriend go?"

There he is! He is flying!

He decided to come back to his girlfriend!
He lands on the water.

He says, "Quack, Quack! Where is my girlfriend?"

They found each other again! How sweet!

There are some more traveling birds in that field! They are swans! They are big white birds with long necks. They have black legs.

The gray ones are babies. They eat little plants.
This baby swan is so hungry!

Now the baby is tired.

He sits down to rest for a while.

Look Aqelesiya! Now the swans are flying away!
How beautiful they are when they fly!

What a wonderful adventure we are having today!

Now it is time for bed.
Tomorrow is a happy new day!

AUTHOR INFORMATION

Linda Dillon deJong is a nature photographer and stained-glass artist living on Camano Island in Washington State. Linda is a Mom to many children gathered from all over the world. After she became a Grandmother, Linda had the idea to write nature photography books to teach children to love our natural world that is full of amazing birds, plants and animals. Linda wants to encourage all children to get outside and experience the wonders of nature.

Lindaglass22@gmail.com